Problem Solving
Workbook

with Reading Strategies

Harcourt Brace & Company

Orlando • Atlanta • Austin • Boston • San Francisco • Chicago • Dallas • New York • Toronto • London

http://www.hbschool.com

CONTENTS

One-to-One Correspondence

I.

2.

3.

4.

Choose the best hat.
Draw one hat for each person.

More and Fewer

1.

2.

Draw more windows on the house.
Draw fewer windows on the house.

Numbers Through 5

_____ 2

_____ 4

_____ 5

_____ 3

_____ 1

Count how many objects
each person is juggling.
Write the number of objects.

PS6   PROBLEM SOLVING

Numbers Through 9

 7

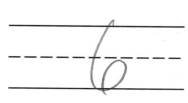 9

 8

 6

Count how many of each.
Write the number.

PROBLEM SOLVING PS7

Name _____

Ten

	Guess	Check		Guess	Check
	9	✓		10	✓
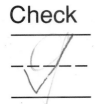	10	✓		10	

Guess how many of each.
Then count to check your answer.

Name _____

Greater Than

Inside   Outside

1.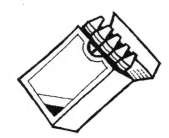

2.

3.

4.

5.

Write how many are inside and how many are outside.
Circle the number that is greater.

Less Than

Color orange the group of vegetables that has I less than the group of pumpkins.
Color red the group of vegetables that has I less than the group of peppers.
Color green the group of vegetables that has I less than the group of tomatoes.

PS10   PROBLEM SOLVING

Harcourt Brace School Publishers

Modeling Addition Story Problems

Draw 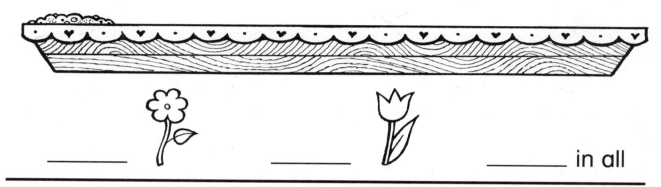 and 🌷.
Write how many in all.

1. Show one way to make 3.

_____ 🌼   _____ 🌷   _____ in all

2. Show one way to make 6.

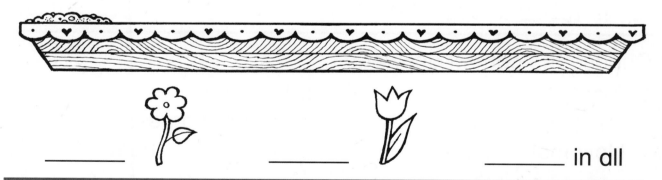

_____ 🌼   _____ 🌷   _____ in all

Make up an addition story.
How many in all? Mark your answer.

3.

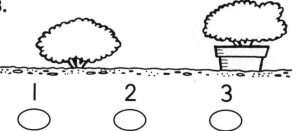

1   2   3

○   ○   ○

4.

4   5   6

○   ○   ○

Adding 1

Draw 1 more.
Write the sum.

1. 1 fish.
   1 more comes.

$1 + 1 = \underline{\ 2\ }$ fish

---

2. 3 cats.
   1 more comes.

$3 + 1 = \underline{\ 4\ }$ cats

Choose the correct answer.

3. 5 ducks.
   1 more comes.
   How many ducks?

5   6
◯   ⬭

4. 4 sheep.
   1 more comes.
   How many sheep?

4   5
◯   ⬭

Harcourt Brace School Publishers

Adding 2

Draw 2 more.
Write the sum.

1. 1 cow.
2 more come.

$1 + 2 = \underline{3}$ cows

2. 2 bears.
2 more come.

$2 + 2 = \underline{}$ bears

Choose the correct answer.

3. Which hat has 2 more
than 1?

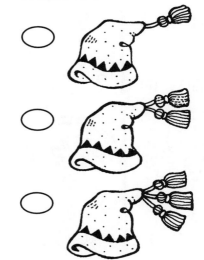

4. Which bunch has 2 more
than 3?

Using Pictures to Add

Draw a picture.
Write the sum.

1. 2 birds sit.
   3 birds eat.
   How many in all?

   $2 + 3 = $ ___5___ birds

2. 2 dogs run.
   2 dogs jump.
   How many in all?

   $2 + 2 = $ _____ dogs

3. 5 cows eat.
   1 cow sleeps.
   How many in all?

   $5 + 1 = $ _____ cows

Mark your answer.

4. 3 frogs hop.
   3 frogs sit.
   How many in all?

   4   5   6
   ⃝   ⃝   ⃝

5. 3 cats sit.
   2 cats sleep.
   How many in all?

   4   5   6
   ⃝   ⃝   ⃝

Harcourt Brace School Publishers

Reading Strategy • Use Pictures Clues

Using pictures can help you solve problems.

2 planes on the ground.
3 planes in the air.
How many in all?

Look at the
picture.

1. Count the planes
   on the ground.

   ___2___ planes

2. Count the planes
   in the air.

   _____ planes

3. Write the addition sentence.

   ___ + ___ = ___ planes

Solve.

4. 2 jets on the ground.
   2 jets in the air.
   How many in all?

   ___ + ___ = ___ jets

5. 3 planes on the ground.
   1 plane in the air.
   How many in all?

   ___ + ___ = ___ planes

Modeling Subtraction Story Problems

Make up a subtraction story problem.
Write how many.

1.

___4___ balloons   ___2___ pop   ___2___ are left

2.

_____ snow people   _____ melts   _____ are left

3.

_____ toy boats   _____ sink   _____ are left

Make up a subtraction story problem.
How many are left? Mark your answer.

4.

○ 3   ○ 4

○ 5   ○ 6

5.

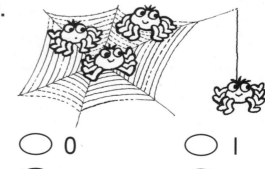

○ 0   ○ l

○ 2   ○ 3

Subtracting 1

Cross out 1.
Write how many are left.

1. There are 4 apples.
Jon eats 1.

How many are left?

$4 - 1 = \underline{3}$ apples

---

2. There are 6 pears.
Nancy eats 1.

How many are left?

$6 - 1 = \underline{}$ pears

---

3. There are 2 apples.
Nat eats 1.
How many are left?

 1   2

○ 3   ○ 4

4. There are 3 oranges.
Angel eats 1.
How many are left?

○ 0   ○ 1

○ 2   ○ 3

Subtracting 2

Cross out pictures to show
the subtraction sentence.
Write how many are left.

1. 4 bugs are on a leaf.
   2 fly away.
   How many are left?

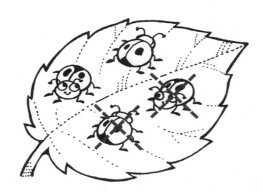

$4 - 2 =$ ___2___ bugs

2. 5 birds are on a fence.
   2 fly away.
   How many are left?

$5 - 2 =$ _____ birds

Choose the correct answer.

3. Which flag has 2 fewer
   than 6 stars?

4. Which animal has 2
   fewer than 4 legs?

Writing Subtraction Sentences

Draw a picture.
Write the number sentence.

1. Pete has 5 balloons. 3 blow away. How many are left? $5 - 3 = \underline{\ 2\ }$ balloons	
2. Kathy has 6 balloons. She gives 3 away. How many are left? $6 - 3 = \underline{\quad}$ balloons	
3. Mia has 4 balloons. 1 pops. How many are left? $4 - 1 = \underline{\quad}$ balloons	

Which subtraction sentence tells how many are left?
Mark your answer.

4.

- ○ $5 - 4 = 1$
- ○ $5 - 3 = 2$
- ○ $5 - 2 = 3$
- ○ $5 - 1 = 4$

5.

- ○ $4 - 0 = 4$
- ○ $4 - 1 = 3$
- ○ $4 - 3 = 1$
- ○ $4 - 4 = 0$

Reading Strategy • Use Word Clues

Read the problem.
Look for word clues.
Solve the problem.

1. 4 dogs play.
   2 **run away**.
   How many are left?

There are ___2___ dogs left.

2. 4 dogs play.
   2 **more** come.
   How many in all?

There are ___6___ dogs in all.

Solve.

3. 6 kittens in a basket.
   3 get out.
   How many are left?

There are _____ kittens left.

4. 1 puppy sleeps.
   5 more come.
   How many in all?

There are _____ puppies in all.

Order Property

Write a number sentence to solve
each problem.

1. Lee has 2 green pens.
   She buys 1 red pen.
   How many pens does
   Lee have?

   $\underline{2} + \underline{1} = \underline{3}$

2. Tim has 1 green pen.
   He buys 2 red pens.
   How many pens does
   Tim have?

   $\underline{} + \underline{} = \underline{}$

3. Sal draws 1 red star.
   She draws 3 blue stars.
   How many stars does
   Sal draw?

   $\underline{} + \underline{} = \underline{}$

4. Laura draws 3 red stars.
   She draws 1 blue star.
   How many stars does
   Laura draw?

   $\underline{} + \underline{} = \underline{}$

Choose the two number sentences
that show you can add in any order.

5. ◯ $3 + 1 = 4$
   $1 + 3 = 4$

   ◯ $3 + 1 = 4$
   $2 + 2 = 4$

   ◯ not here

6. ◯ $1 + 1 = 2$
   $2 + 2 = 4$

   ◯ $2 + 4 = 6$
   $3 + 3 = 6$

   ◯ $2 + 4 = 6$
   $4 + 2 = 6$

Harcourt Brace School Publishers

Addition Combinations

Draw a picture.
Write the number sentence.

1. Jack sees 4 red birds.
   Jane sees 3 yellow birds.
   How many birds in all?

   $\underline{\ \ 4\ \ } + \underline{\ \ 3\ \ } = \underline{\ \ 7\ \ }$ birds

2. 3 birds eat seeds.
   5 more come.
   How many birds in all?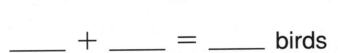

   $\underline{\ \ \ \ } + \underline{\ \ \ \ } = \underline{\ \ \ \ }$ birds

3. I bird takes a bath.
   6 more come.
   How many birds in all?

   $\underline{\ \ \ \ } + \underline{\ \ \ \ } = \underline{\ \ \ \ }$ birds

Mark the correct answer.

4. Which is a way to
   make 7?

   ○ 3 + 2
   ○ 2 + 4
   ○ 0 + 7
   ○ I + 7

5. Which is a way to
   make 8?

   ○ 4 + 4
   ○ 6 + I
   ○ 2 + 4
   ○ 3 + 4

More Addition Combinations

Draw a picture.
Write the number sentence.

1. Stan reads 4 books.
   Tony reads 5 books.
   How many books in all?

   ___4___ + ___5___ = ___9___ books

2. Mia checks out 2 books.
   Zack checks out 6 books.
   How many books in all?

   _____ + _____ = _____ books

3. 7 books are on the shelf.
   2 books are on the desk.
   How many books in all?

   _____ + _____ = _____ books

Mark the correct answer.

4. The sum of two numbers is 9. Which are the two numbers?

   ○ 4 and 4
   ○ 3 and 6
   ○ 7 and 1
   ○ 3 and 5

5. There are 10 children at a party. Which tells how many girls and boys there are?

   ○ 3 girls and 3 boys
   ○ 5 girls and 4 boys
   ○ 3 girls and 6 boys
   ○ 7 girls and 3 boys

Horizontal and Vertical Addition

Write the problem two ways.

1. Ned has 6 fish.
He buys 4 more.
How many fish in all?

__10__ fish

$6 + 4 = 10$

$$\begin{array}{r} 6 \\ +\ 4 \\ \hline 10 \end{array}$$

2. Alice has 3 pennies.
She gets 6 more.
How many pennies in all?

_____ pennies

___ + ___ = ___

$$\begin{array}{r} \underline{} \\ +\ \underline{} \\ \hline \underline{} \end{array}$$

Mark the correct answer.

3. Pam writes this addition sentence.

$$3 + 5 = 8$$

Which problem is the same?

○ $\begin{array}{r} 3 \\ +4 \\ \hline 7 \end{array}$ ○ $\begin{array}{r} 3 \\ +5 \\ \hline 8 \end{array}$ ○ $\begin{array}{r} 4 \\ +4 \\ \hline 8 \end{array}$

4. Ali writes this problem.

$$\begin{array}{r} 4 \\ +5 \\ \hline 9 \end{array}$$

Which addition sentence is the same?

○ $4 + 5 = 9$

○ $4 + 4 = 8$

○ $5 + 2 = 7$

○ $6 + 3 = 9$

Harcourt Brace School Publishers

Reading Strategy • Using Pictures

Using pictures can help you solve problems.

Tammy buys a top.
She buys a doll.
How much does she spend?

1. Look at the pictures.
   Write the answer.
   How much does the top cost?   ___4___ ¢

   How much does the doll cost?   _____ ¢

2. Write an addition sentence.
   Solve the problem.

   ___¢ + ___¢ = ___¢

Solve.

3. Jim buys a boat.
   He buys a car.
   How much does
   he spend?

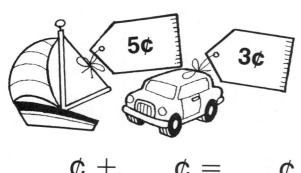

   ___¢ + ___¢ = ___¢

4. Amy buys a ball.
   She buys jacks.
   How much does she
   spend?

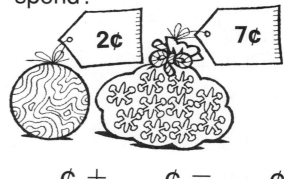

   ___¢ + ___¢ = ___¢

Counting On 1 and 2

Count on to add.
Write the sum.

1.

6 birds in a house.
1 more comes.
How many birds in all?

$6 + 1 = \underline{\quad 7 \quad}$ birds

2.

8 bees in a hive.
2 more come.
How many bees in all?

$8 + 2 = \underline{\qquad}$ bees

3.

3 bears in a cave.
2 more come.
How many bears in all?

$3 + 2 = \underline{\qquad}$ bears

Mark the correct answer.

4. Which has same sum?

$1 + 2 = \underline{\qquad}$

- ◯ 1 + 1
- ◯ 2 + 1
- ◯ 3 + 1
- ◯ 4 + 1

5. Which has same sum?

$4 + 2 = \underline{\qquad}$

- ◯ 4 + 1
- ◯ 3 + 3
- ◯ 5 + 0
- ◯ 2 + 2

Counting On 3

Count on to add.
Write the sum.

1.

Jan has 4 pennies.
She gets 3 more.
How many pennies in all?

$4 + 3 = \underline{\quad 7 \quad}$ pennies

2.

Dave has 8 pennies.
He gets 2 more.
How many pennies in all?

$8 + 2 = \underline{\qquad}$ pennies

3.

Rick 6 pennies.
He gets 3 more.
How many pennies in all?

$6 + 3 = \underline{\qquad}$ pennies

Mark the correct answer.

4. Which is a way to make 4?

○ 3 + 1
○ 3 + 2
○ 1 + 2
○ 4 + 2

5. Which is a way to make 8?

○ 5 + 1
○ 5 + 3
○ 5 + 2
○ 5 + 4

Doubles

Write a number sentence.

1. Annie has 5 crayons.
   Max has the same number.
   How many do they have in all?

   __5__ + __5__ = __10__ crayons

2. Jill has 4 pens.
   Nick has 4 more than Jill.
   How many does Nick have?

   ____ + ____ = ____ pens

Mark the correct answer.

3. Which doubles fact goes
   with the picture?

   ◯ 1 + 1 = 2
   ◯ 2 + 2 = 4
   ◯ 3 + 3 = 6
   ◯ 4 + 4 = 8

4. Which doubles fact goes
   with the picture?

   ◯ 2 + 2 = 4
   ◯ 3 + 3 = 6
   ◯ 4 + 4 = 8
   ◯ 5 + 5 = 10

Addition Facts Practice

Draw a picture.
Solve.

1. A bike has 2 wheels.
A car has 4 wheels.
How many wheels in all?

____6____ wheels

2. A wagon has 4 wheels.
How many wheels do
2 wagons have?

_____ wheels

3. A truck has 6 wheels.
A van has 4 wheels.
How many wheels in all?

_____ wheels

Mark the correct answer.

4. Which is a doubles fact?

○ 2 + 3 = 5
○ 2 + 2 = 4
○ 4 + 2 = 6

5. Which is **not** a doubles fact?

○ 4 + 3 = 7
○ 3 + 3 = 6
○ 4 + 4 = 8

Name _____

Reading Strategy • Use Word Clues

Using word clues can help
you solve problems.

Read the problem.
Look for word clues.
Draw a picture.
Solve.

1. Tom has **6 plants.**
   He **gives 2 away**.
   How many are left?

   There are ___4___ plants left.

2. **3 plants** are **big**.
   2 plants are **little**.
   How many plants in all?

   _____ plants

3. Toby has 2 big plants.
   He buys 4 little plants.
   How many plants in all?

   _____ plants

4. Mike picks 5 flowers.
   He gives 3 away.
   How many are left?

   _____ flowers

Facts Practice

Draw a picture.
Write the number sentence.

1. Carla has 7 leaves.
   She drops 3.
   How many leaves are left?

   __7__ − __3__ = __4__ leaves

2. Jim has 4 shells.
   He finds 2 more.
   How many shells in all?

   ____ + ____ = ____ shells

3. Pete has 8 nuts.
   He finds 1 more.
   How many nuts in all?

   ____ + ____ = ____ nuts

Mark the correct answer.

4. Which number names
   the sum?

   $8 + 2 =$ _____

   ◯ 10
   ◯ 9
   ◯ 8

5. Which number names the
   difference?

   $10 − 2 =$ _____

   ◯ 10
   ◯ 9
   ◯ 8

Reading Strategy • Use Word Clues and Pictures

Using word clues and pictures can help you solve problems.

Read the problem.
Look for word clues.
Look at the picture.
Cross out the frogs that hop away.
Solve.

1. 5 frogs sit on a log.
   2 **hop away**.
   How many now?

   5 − 2 = __3__ frogs

Solve.

2. 6 fish swim in a group.
   4 swim away.
   How many now?

_____ fish

3. 3 crabs sit on the bottom.
   3 more come.
   How many now?

_____ crabs

Inside, Outside, On

Draw a picture.
Solve.

1. Tom draws a nest.
   He draws 2 birds **inside** the nest.
   He draws 1 bird **on** the nest.
   He draws 2 birds **outside**
   the nest. How many birds in all?

   _____5_____ birds

2. Simon draws a rectangle.
   He draws a circle **inside**
   the rectangle.
   He draws a square that is
   outside the circle but
   inside the rectangle.
   Show what Simon draws.

Mark the correct answer.

3. Where is the man?

   ◯ inside the car
   ◯ on the car
   ◯ outside the car

4. Where is
   the bird?

   ◯ inside the birdhouse
   ◯ on the birdhouse
   ◯ outside the birdhouse

Reading Strategy • Use Word Clues

Use the position words **left** and
right to find where the friends will meet.

1. Find the X.
2. Walk right until you see
   the bench.
3. Turn and walk to the right
   of the slide.
4. Turn left at the tree.
5. Walk until you see me.

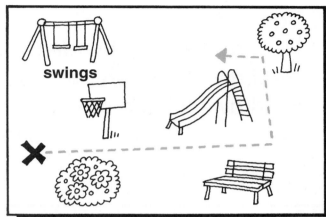

swings

left   **right**

1. Read all the directions.
   Look for the position words **left** and **right**.

2. Follow each direction. Use the position words.
   Mark the path you would take.

3. Solve the problem. Where will the friends meet?

   _____

   _ _ _ _ _ _ _ _ _ _ _ _ _ _ _

   _____

Solve.

4. Draw a picture of your
   playground.
   Draw yourself to the
   right of your favorite
   place to play.

Harcourt Brace School Publishers

Reproducing and Extending Patterns

Draw and color these patterns.

1. Marie uses red blocks
   to make the pattern triangle,
   square, circle. Draw her
   pattern two times.

2. Tom uses cubes to make
   the pattern yellow, red,
   red. Draw his pattern
   two times.

3. Jeff uses red squares and
   blue circles to make the
   pattern square, circle, circle.
   Draw his pattern two times.

Mark the correct answer.

4. What shape comes next?

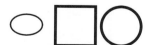

5. Which shows the pattern
   square, triangle?

Making and Extending Patterns

Draw and color these patterns.

1. Glenn has 3 circles,
   3 squares, and 3 triangles.
   Show a pattern he can make.

2. Arlene has 3 circles and 6 cubes.
   Show a pattern she can make.

3. Carol uses green circles, red squares,
   and blue triangles to make the pattern
   square, triangle, circle.
   Draw her pattern three times.

Mark the correct answer.

4. Find a different pattern
   that uses the same
   shapes as this one.

5. Which shapes come next
   in the pattern?

Reading Strategy • Make Predictions

Making predictions can help you solve problems.

Ruth makes this pattern with beads.
There is a mistake in the pattern.
What mistake do you see?

1. Look at the pattern.
   What is the pattern rule?

square, triangle, triangle

2. Use the pattern rule.
   Say the first 7 shapes
   in Ruth's pattern.

3. Make a prediction.
   What comes next in the pattern?
   Circle the mistake.
   Draw the correct pattern.

Find the pattern rule. Circle the mistake.
Make a prediction and continue the pattern.

4. Tim makes this block
   pattern. Circle the mistake.
   Draw the correct pattern.

5. Nora makes this bead
   pattern. Circle the mistake.
   Draw the correct pattern.

Harcourt Brace School Publishers

READING STRATEGY   PS59

Counting On to 12

Draw how many come.
Write the sum.

1. 8 children are in the
   playhouse. 2 more come.
   How many children in all?

   __8__ + __2__ = __10__

2. 8 children are in the sub.
   3 more come.
   How many children in all?

   ____ + ____ = ____

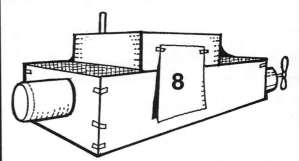

3. 9 children make a snow fort.
   3 more come.
   How many children in all?

   ____ + ____ = ____

Mark the correct answer.

4. Count on.
   Which number is the sum?

   $9 + 2 =$ _____

   ◯ 11   ◯ 13

   ◯ 12   ◯ 14

5. Count on. Which
   numbers have the
   sum 11?

   ◯ 3 + 9   ◯ 9 + 2

   ◯ 8 + 2   ◯ 2 + 3

Harcourt Brace School Publishers

Relating Addition and Subtraction

Write a number sentence.
Solve.

1. Nora has 5 apples. She picks 2 more. How many apples does she have in all?	$\underline{5} \; \oplus \; \underline{2} = \underline{7}$ apples
2. Nora has 7 apples. She eats 2. How many apples does she have left?	$\underline{\hphantom{0}} \; \ominus \; \underline{\hphantom{0}} = \underline{\hphantom{0}}$ apples
3. Bob has 9 plums. He eats 1. How many plums does he have left?	$\underline{\hphantom{0}} \; \ominus \; \underline{\hphantom{0}} = \underline{\hphantom{0}}$ plums

Mark the correct answer.

4. The sum of two numbers
   is 9. One number is 6.
   What is the other number?

   ○ 2
   ○ 3
   ○ 4
   ○ not here

5. The sum of two numbers
   is 12. One number is 5.
   What is the other number?

   ○ 7
   ○ 6
   ○ 5
   ○ not here

Counting Back

Count back or count on to solve.

1. Betty stands on number 6.
   She takes 2 hops back.
   What number is she on now?

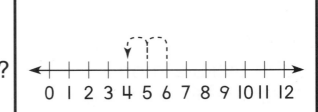

2. Ann stands on number 8.
   She takes 3 hops forward.
   What number is she on now?

   _____

3. Stan stands on number 11.
   He takes 3 hops back.
   What number is he on now?

   _____

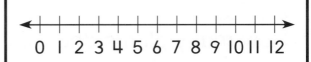

Mark the correct answer.

4. Count back.
   Which is the difference?

   $9 - 2 =$ _____
   ○ 7
   ○ 8
   ○ 9
   ○ 10

5. Count on.
   Which is the sum?

   $9 + 2 =$ _____
   ○ 10
   ○ 11
   ○ 12
   ○ 13

Harcourt Brace School Publishers

Compare to Subtract

Draw a picture.
Solve.

1. There are 12 children in line.
   The bus has 8 seats.
   How many fewer seats than
   children are there?

   __4__ fewer seats

2. There are 9 people waiting
   for the bus. The bus has
   7 empty seats.
   How many more people
   than seats are there?

   _____ more people

Mark the correct answer.

3. Which question goes with
   the problem?
   There are 8 children.
   4 children leave.

   ○ How many children
     in all?

   ○ How many children
     are left?

   ○ How many more
     children are there?

4. Which question goes with
   the problem?
   There are 9 children.
   3 more children come.

   ○ How many children
     in all?

   ○ How many children
     are left?

   ○ How many fewer
     children are there?

Fact Families

Draw a picture.
Write the number sentence.

1. Martha has 5 red blocks.
She has 3 blue blocks.
How many blocks does
Martha have?

$$\underline{5} \oplus \underline{3} = \underline{8}$$
blocks

2. Toby has 8 cars.
He gives 3 cars to his sister.
How many cars does Toby
have left?

$$\underline{} \ominus \underline{} = \underline{}$$
cars

3. Jan lines up 6 number cards.
She counts back 3 cards
from 6. On what number
does she stop?

_____

Mark the correct answer.

4. Which number sentence
belongs in this fact family?

$$8 + 3 = 11$$

○ $8 + 4 = 12$
○ $8 + 2 = 10$
○ $11 - 4 = 7$
○ $11 - 3 = 8$

5. Which number sentence
belongs in this fact family?

$$5 + 5 = 10$$

○ $10 - 0 = 10$
○ $10 - 5 = 5$
○ $6 + 6 = 12$
○ $6 + 4 = 10$

Reading Strategy • Use Word Clues

Using word clues such as **more** and **fewer** can
help you use pictures to estimate.

Look at the sheep.
Which is the better estimate?

more than 10   fewer than 10

---

1. Read the problem. Think about the
meaning of **more** and **fewer**.

more than 10   10   fewer than 10

---

2. Estimate the number of sheep.

Think: 1 group of 10 sheep and 3 more sheep.
There are **more than 10** sheep.

Circle the better estimate.

3.

more than 10

fewer than 10

4.

more than 10

fewer than 10

Ordinals

first | second | third | fourth | fifth | sixth | seventh | eighth

Use the picture to find the answer.

1. Lynn takes the seventh animal to school. What animal does she take?

2. Lynn counts all the animals that come after the third animal. How many are there?

_____

3. Lynn adds a toy frog at the end of the line. In what position is the frog?

_____

_____

4. Lynn puts a toy cow between the duck and the hen. In what position is the hen now?

_____

_____

Mark the correct answer.

5. The winner in a race crosses the finish line

_____.

○ first   ○ second
○ third   ○ fourth

6. There are nine seats left in a movie theater. You are the tenth in line. Will you get a seat?

○ yes   ○ no

Harcourt Brace School Publishers

Counting by Tens

Draw a picture.
Count by tens.

1. There are 4 children in a family.
   Each child gets 10 dollars for
   a present. How much money
   do they get in all?

   __40__ dollars

2. Carlos has 7 packs of baseball
   cards. Each pack has 10 cards.
   How many cards does he have
   in all?

   _____ cards

Mark the correct answer.

3. What three numbers
   come next in this
   pattern?

   20, 30, 40, ___, ___, ___

   ○ 41, 42, 43
   ○ 45, 50, 55
   ○ 60, 70, 80
   ○ 50, 60, 70

4. How many in all?

   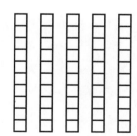

   ○ 5
   ○ 40
   ○ 50
   ○ 60

Counting by Fives

Draw a picture.
Skip-count to solve.

1. Hannah is 6 years old today.
Her grandmother gives her
5 dollars for each year. How
much money does Hannah get?

   __30__ dollars

2. Tory builds 8 towers.
He uses 10 blocks in each tower.
How many blocks does Tory use
in all?

   _____ blocks

Mark the correct answer.

3. How many in all?

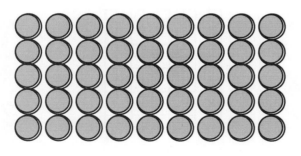

   ○ 9
   ○ 40
   ○ 45
   ○ 90

4. What three numbers
come next in this pattern?

   55, 60, 65, ___, ___, ___

   ○ 80, 85, 90
   ○ 75, 80, 85
   ○ 70, 80, 90
   ○ 70, 75, 80

Counting by Twos

Draw a picture.
Skip-count to solve.

1. Doug thinks of a number.
   It is between 35 and 40.
   It is 2 more than 36.
   What is Doug's number?

   <u>38</u>

2. Sal thinks of a number.
   It is between 70 and 80.
   It is 5 more than 70.
   What is Sal's number?

   _____

Mark the correct answer.

3. When you say every
   second number, you are
   counting by _____.

   ○ twos
   ○ fives
   ○ tens

4. What three numbers
   come next in this
   pattern?

   52, 54, 56, ___, ___, ___

   ○ 57, 59, 61
   ○ 58, 60, 62
   ○ 60, 65, 70

Even and Odd Numbers

Draw a picture to solve.
Then circle **odd** or **even.**

1. Marissa plants 5 flowers.
   She plants 3 more. How many
   flowers does she plant?

   __8__ flowers   odd (even)

2. Bill mows 3 lawns on Monday.
   He mows double that number
   on Tuesday. How many lawns
   does he mow on both days?

   _____ lawns   odd   even

3. 6 children each plant 2 bulbs.
   How many bulbs do they
   plant in all?

   _____ bulbs   odd   even

Mark the correct answer.

4. The sum of an even
   number and an odd
   number is always _____.

   ⭕ even   ⭕ odd

5. The sum of two odd
   numbers is always
   _____.

   ⭕ even   ⭕ odd

Harcourt Brace School Publishers

Pennies and Nickels

Draw a picture. Count.
Write the amount.

1. Lisa has 2 pennies.
   She finds 3 more pennies in a jar.
   How much money does Lisa
   have in all?

   _____5___ ¢

2. Bob has 2 nickels.
   His mom gives him 1 more nickel.
   How much money does he have
   in all?

   _____ ¢

Mark the correct answer.

3. Which group of coins is
   worth more?

   ◯ 6 pennies

   ◯ 2 nickels

   ◯ 11 pennies

4. Hanna wants to count
   her coins. What should
   she say?

   ◯ 1¢, 2¢, 3¢, 4¢

   ◯ 5¢, 10¢, 15¢

   ◯ 5¢, 10¢, 15¢, 20¢

Pennies and Dimes

Draw a picture. Count.
Write the amount.

1. Ned has 4 dimes.
   He earns 2 more dimes.
   How much money does Ned
   have in all?

   _60_ ¢

2. Patty has 2 nickels.
   She earns 3 more nickels.
   How much money does she
   have in all?

   _____ ¢

Mark the correct answer.

3. Mary has these coins.

   How much money does
   she have?

   ◯ 2¢   ◯ 10¢
   ◯ 15¢   ◯ 20¢

4. Ben wants to count
   his coins. What should
   he say?

   ◯ 1¢, 2¢, 3¢
   ◯ 5¢, 10¢, 15¢
   ◯ 10¢, 20¢, 30¢
   ◯ not here

Harcourt Brace School Publishers

Counting Collections of Nickels and Pennies

Draw a picture. Count.
Write the amount.

1. Dan has 3 nickels in his bank.
He puts in 4 pennies.
How much money does Dan
have in all?

   ___19___ ¢

2. Jessica has 2 dimes.
Her aunt gives her 3 more dimes.
How much money does
Jessica have in all?

   _____ ¢

Mark the correct answer.

3. Which group of coins is
worth the most?

   ○ 3 nickels and
      3 pennies

   ○ 2 nickels and
      9 pennies

   ○ 4 nickels and
      1 penny

   ○ 3 nickels and
      7 pennies

4. Which amount do these
coins add up to?

   ○ 10¢   ○ 12¢

   ○ 22¢   ○ not here

Counting Collections of Dimes and Pennies

Draw a picture. Count.
Write the amount.

1. Katie has 3 dimes.
   Her mom puts 2 more dimes
   in her lunch box. How much
   money does Katie have in all?

   _50_ ¢

2. John has 4 nickels in his bank.
   He puts in 4 pennies.
   How much money does he have
   in all?

   _____ ¢

Mark the correct answer.

3. Which group of coins is
   worth the least?

   ◯ 12 pennies

   ◯ 1 dime 1 penny

   ◯ 1 dime 4 pennies

   ◯ 2 dimes

4. What amount do these
   coins add up to?

   ◯ 5¢   ◯ 13¢

   ◯ 23¢   ◯ 50¢

Reading Strategy • Use Pictures

Using pictures can help you
solve problems.

A toy truck costs 21¢.
Which coins could Thomas
use to buy the truck?

1. Look at the picture.
   Put the coins into groups.
   Then find the value for each group.

dimes	nickels	pennies
__20__ ¢	__10__ ¢	__2__ ¢

2. Write the number of coins from the groups
   that add up to the price of the toy truck.

   __1__ dime   __2__ nickels   __1__ penny = __21__ ¢

Solve.

3.

   A toy bus costs 12¢.
   Which coins could you
   use to buy it?

   _____ dime

   _____ nickels

   _____ pennies

Trading Pennies, Nickels, and Dimes

Use the fewest coins.
Draw the coins.
Solve.

1. Mrs. Polt needs dimes for parking. She has 20 pennies and 2 nickels. How many dimes can she trade for?

___3___ dimes

2. Mr. Miller uses dimes and nickels for tolls. He has 35 pennies. How many dimes and nickels can he trade for?

_____ dimes   _____ nickel

Mark the correct answer.

3. What are the fewest coins you can use to show 25¢?

○ 2 coins

○ 3 coins

○ 5 coins

○ 25 coins

4. Tina has 4 coins. José has 8 coins. Who has more money?

○ Tina

○ José

○ You cannot tell.

Harcourt Brace School Publishers

Equal Amounts

Draw a picture.
Write the amount.

1. Jill buys jacks that cost 30¢.
   Show two ways she could pay.

   __ dimes __ nickels __ pennies

   __ dimes __ nickels __ pennies

2. Alex buys a ball that costs 45¢.
   Show two ways he could pay.

   __ dimes __ nickels __ pennies

   __ dimes __ nickels __ pennies

Mark the correct answer.

3. Betty and Frank have the
   same amount of money.
   Betty has only dimes.
   Frank has only nickels.
   Who has fewer coins?

   ○ Betty

   ○ Frank

   ○ You cannot tell.

4. Joe and Carmen have
   the same number of
   coins. Do they have the
   same amount of money?

   ○ yes

   ○ no

   ○ You cannot tell.

How Much Is Needed?

Draw a picture.
Solve.

1. Nicky has 22¢ in her purse.
   She has 4 coins.
   What are they?

   _2_ dimes _0_ nickels _2_ pennies

2. Don has 1 dime and 7 nickels.
   Lisa has the same amount but
   fewer coins. What coins does
   she have?

   __ dimes __ nickel

Mark the correct answer.

3. Ted uses fewer coins
   than Janna to show the
   same amount.
   This means that some of
   Ted's coins are worth

   _____.

   ○ more

   ○ less

   ○ the same

4. A cookie costs 15¢. Joe
   uses the fewest coins to
   buy it. What coins does
   he use?

   ○ 15 pennies

   ○ 2 nickels and
     5 pennies

   ○ 3 nickels

   ○ 1 dime and 1 nickel

Quarter

Draw a picture. Count.
Write the amount.

1. Fran has 1 quarter.
   She earns 1 dime and 1 nickel.
   How much money does Fran
   have in all?

   __40__ ¢

2. Pete has 2 dimes.
   He finds 1 more dime and 2
   nickels in his bag. How much
   money does Pete have in all?

   _____ ¢

Mark the correct answer.

3. Which group of coins is
   worth the most?

   ◯ 1 quarter and
     2 dimes

   ◯ 1 quarter and
     3 nickels

   ◯ 1 quarter and
     5 nickels

   ◯ 1 quarter and
     20 pennies

4. What amount do these
   coins add up to?

   ◯ 36¢   ◯ 39¢

   ◯ 41¢   ◯ 46¢

Reading Strategy • Make Predictions

Making predictions can help you
solve problems.

A toy plane costs 37¢. Charlie has
I quarter, I dime, I nickel, and
I penny. Does Charlie have
enough to buy the plane?

1. Use coins to show the
amount Charlie has.
Count two coins.

__25__¢, __35__¢

2. Make a prediction.
Do you think Charlie has
enough to buy the plane?

__yes__

3. Continue counting Charlie's coins to find the value.

_____¢, _____¢, _____¢, _____¢

Make a prediction. Then solve.
Use the fewest coins.

4. A toy bear costs 37¢.
Jill has 2 dimes, 5 nickels,
and 3 pennies. Can Jill
buy the plane?
If so, what coins should
she use?

_____ dimes

_____ nickels

_____ pennies

Ordering Months and Days

January	February	March	April	May	June

S M T W T F S
January: 1 2 3 / 4 5 6 7 8 9 10 / 11 12 13 14 15 16 17 / 18 19 20 21 22 23 24 / 25 26 27 28 29 30 31

February: 1 2 3 4 5 6 7 / 8 9 10 11 12 13 14 / 15 16 17 18 19 20 21 / 22 23 24 25 26 27 28

March: 1 2 3 4 5 6 7 / 8 9 10 11 12 13 14 / 15 16 17 18 19 20 21 / 22 23 24 25 26 27 28 / 29 30 31

April: 1 2 3 4 / 5 6 7 8 9 10 11 / 12 13 14 15 16 17 18 / 19 20 21 22 23 24 25 / 26 27 28 29 30

May: 1 2 / 3 4 5 6 7 8 9 / 10 11 12 13 14 15 16 / 17 18 19 20 21 22 23 / 24 31 25 26 27 28 29 30

June: 1 2 3 4 5 6 / 7 8 9 10 11 12 13 / 14 15 16 17 18 19 20 / 21 22 23 24 25 26 27 / 28 29 30

July	August	September	October	November	December

July: 1 2 3 4 / 5 6 7 8 9 10 11 / 12 13 14 15 16 17 18 / 19 20 21 22 23 24 25 / 26 27 28 29 30 31

August: 1 / 2 3 4 5 6 7 8 / 9 10 11 12 13 14 15 / 16 17 18 19 20 21 22 / 23 30 24 31 25 26 27 28 29

September: 1 2 3 4 5 / 6 7 8 9 10 11 12 / 13 14 15 16 17 18 19 / 20 21 22 23 24 25 26 / 27 28 29 30

October: 1 2 3 / 4 5 6 7 8 9 10 / 11 12 13 14 15 16 17 / 18 19 20 21 22 23 24 / 25 26 27 28 29 30 31

November: 1 2 3 4 5 6 7 / 8 9 10 11 12 13 14 / 15 16 17 18 19 20 21 / 22 23 24 25 26 27 28 / 29 30

December: 1 2 3 4 5 / 6 7 8 9 10 11 12 / 13 14 15 16 17 18 19 / 20 21 22 23 24 25 26 / 27 28 29 30 31

Use the calendar to answer each question.

1. Ann's birthday is in the third month of the year. In what month is her birthday?

_____

2. Tom's birthday comes in the month after June. In what month is Tom's birthday?

_____

_____

3. What is the month before December?

_____

_____

4. What is the ninth month of the year?

_____

_____

Mark the correct answer.

5. How many months are there in one year?

○ 10 months

○ 11 months

○ 12 months

○ not here

6. What month comes between May and July?

○ April

○ June

○ August

○ not here

Reading Strategy • Matching Text

Looking for matching words can help you solve
a problem.

Jon has a game on the second
Monday of November.
On what date is the game?

November

SUN.	MON.	TUES.	WED.	THURS	FRI.	SAT
	1	2	3	4	5	6
7	8	9	10	11	12	13
14	15	16	17	18	19	20
21	22	23	24	25	26	27
28	29	30				

1. Read the problem.
   What date do you
   need to find?

2. Match words from the problem with words
   on the calendar.
   Find **Monday** in the list of days at the top of
   the calendar.

3. Find the second Monday on the calendar.
   What is the date?

November 8

Use the calendar to answer the questions.

4. Linda's party is the third
   Tuesday of November.
   On what date is the party?

   _____

   - - - - - - - - - - - - -

5. Thanksgiving is the fourth
   Thursday of November.
   On what date is
   Thanksgiving?

   _____

   - - - - - - - - - - - - -

Harcourt Brace School Publishers

Ordering Events

Read each story.
Write **morning, afternoon,** or **evening** to tell
the time.

1. Luis is hungry after
   school. He eats an apple
   for a snack. Then he
   goes outside to play.

   afternoon

2. Sally takes too much time
   getting dressed. After
   breakfast, she must run
   to catch the school bus.

   _____

3. Marta takes the bus to
   her music teacher's
   house. She gets home
   before it is dark.

   _____

4. Tammy puts on her
   pajamas. Then she
   reads a story before
   going to sleep.

   _____

Mark the correct answer.

5. Which do most people
   do in the evening?

   ⬭ eat breakfast

   ⬭ eat lunch

   ⬭ eat dinner

6. When does this
   happen?

   ⬭ in the morning

   ⬭ in the afternoon

   ⬭ in the evening

Reading Strategy • Use Prior Knowledge

How much time do these things take to do?
Number them from the shortest time to the longest time.

Leslie makes
her bed.

__2__

Leslie hangs
up her coat.

__1__

Leslie eats
dinner.

__3__

---

1. Read each sentence.
   About how long does it take you to do each thing?

   It takes a very short time to hang up a coat.
   It takes a longer time to make a bed.
   It takes the longest time to eat dinner.

Number these things from the shortest time
to the longest time. Use 1, 2, 3.

2. Mark gets ready for bed.
   He takes a bath.
   He brushes his hair.
   He brushes his teeth.

   _____ He takes a bath.

   _____ He brushes his
   hair.

   _____ He brushes his
   teeth.

Harcourt Brace School Publishers

Reading Strategy • Use Word Clues

Tina paints a (big) picture
for her dad's birthday.
About how long will it
take to paint the picture?

(more than 1 minute)

less than 1 minute

1. Read the problem.
   Draw a line under what you
   want to find out.

2. Circle the word that tells
   about the picture.

3. Estimate how long it will take.
   Circle your estimate.
   Act out the problem to check if needed.

Read the problem. Look for clues
to help you estimate. Circle your
estimate. Then act it out if needed.

4. Tina signs a birthday
   card with her first name.
   About how long will
   it take?

   less than a minute

   more than a minute

5. Jim writes a long
   story about his party.
   About how long will
   it take?

   less than a minute

   more than a minute

Using Nonstandard Units

Draw a picture.
Write how many ⬭ long.

1. Mark uses ⬭ to measure his
pencil. About how many ⬭
long are 2 pencils?

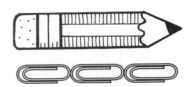

about ___6___ ⬭

2. Jan uses ⬭ to measure a pin.
About how many ⬭ long are
3 pins?

about _____ ⬭

Mark the correct answer.

3. Dan's desk measures
29 paper clips long. Bill's
desk measures 36
paper clips long. Who
has the longer desk?

○ Dan
○ Bill

4. The length of Pam's shoe
is 2 paper clips longer
than Kim's shoe. Who
has the longer shoe?

○ Pam
○ Kim

Measuring in Inch Units

Color the inch units.
Write the number of inches.

1. Diane's ribbon is 6 inches long.
   Kara's ribbon is 4 inches shorter.
   How long is Kara's ribbon?

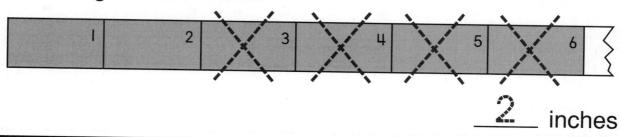

__2__ inches

2. Adam's string is 3 inches long.
   Pat's string is 2 inches longer.
   How long is Pat's string?

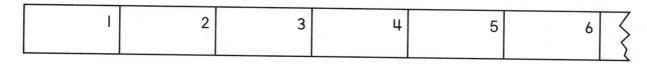

_____ inches

Mark the correct answer.

3. Each link of a chain is
   1 inch. The chain has
   7 links. How long is
   the chain?

   ○ 5 inches
   ○ 6 inches
   ○ 7 inches
   ○ 8 inches

4. A toy robot takes 10 equal
   steps to walk a 10-inch
   line. How long is the
   robot's foot?

   ○ 1 inch
   ○ 2 inches
   ○ 4 inches
   ○ 5 inches

Using an Inch Ruler

Draw a line to show where to cut.

1. Sarah needs a ribbon 5 inches long.
Draw a line to show where you would
cut the ribbon.

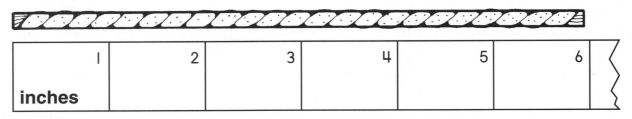

2. Diane needs a piece of yarn 3 inches long.
Draw a line to show where you would cut
the yarn.

Mark the correct answer.

3. How long is it?

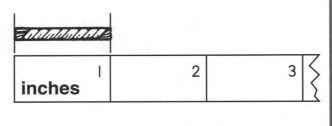

 ○ 2 inches

 ○ 1 inch

 ○ 3 inches

4. How long is it?

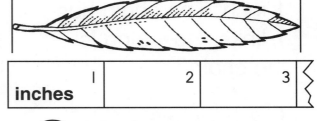

 ○ 1 inch

 ○ 2 inches

 ○ 3 inches

Measuring in Centimeter Units

Color the centimeter units.
Write how many.

1. A crayon is 6 centimeters long.
   A rubber band is 2 centimeters shorter.
   How long is the rubber band?

| 1 | 2 | 3 | 4 | 5 | 6 | 7 | 8 | 9 | 10 | 11 | 12 | 13 | 14 | 15 |

___4___ centimeters

2. A pen is 10 centimeters long.
   A marker is 2 centimeters longer.
   How long is the marker?

| 1 | 2 | 3 | 4 | 5 | 6 | 7 | 8 | 9 | 10 | 11 | 12 | 13 | 14 | 15 |

_____ centimeters

Mark the correct answer.

3. How many inches long?

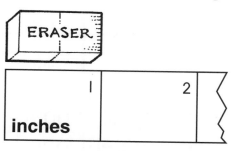

- ○ 1 inch
- ○ 2 inches
- ○ 3 inches
- ○ 4 inches

4. How many centimeters long?

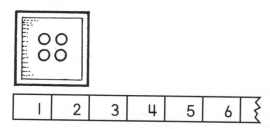

- ○ 2 centimeters
- ○ 3 centimeters
- ○ 4 centimeters
- ○ 5 centimeters

Using a Centimeter Ruler

Draw a line to show the centimeters.

1. Mrs. Miller wants to cut
   8 centimeters of lace.

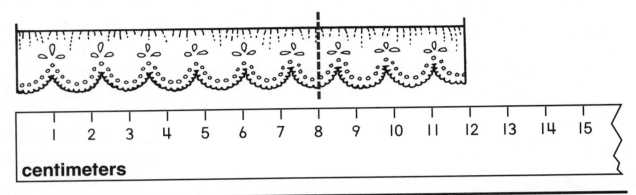

2. Mr. Polt wants to cut
   12 centimeters of wood.

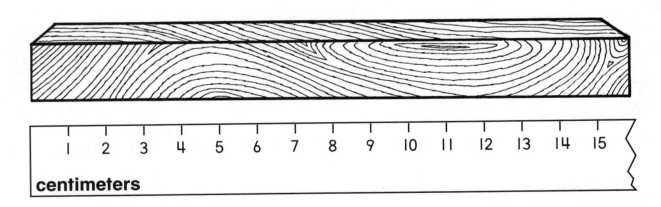

Mark the correct answer.

3. Which object is about
   8 centimeters long?

  ◯ your math book

  ◯ a crayon

  ◯ a paper clip

4. Which object is about
   15 centimeters long?

  ◯ a paintbrush

  ◯ a key

  ◯ a safety pin

Harcourt Brace School Publishers

Using a Balance

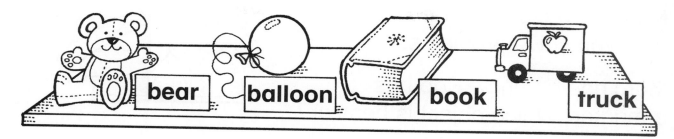

bear   balloon   book   truck

Use the picture. Write the answer.

1. Leslie takes something to share for show-and-tell. She chooses the heaviest object on the shelf.

What does she choose?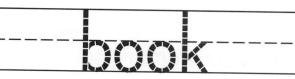

2. Rob takes something to share for show-and-tell. He chooses the lightest object on the shelf.

What does he choose? _____

Mark the correct answer.

3. A paper clip is heavier than a pin. A penny is heavier than a paper clip. Which object is heaviest?

○ paper clip

○ pin

○ penny

4. A shoe is lighter than a book. A tube of paint is lighter than a shoe. Which object is lightest?

○ shoe

○ book

○ tube of paint

Reading Strategy • Make a Prediction

Making predictions can
help you solve problems.

Marc has a pencil. Rob has
a marker. Which object is heavier?

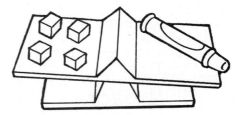

1. About how many 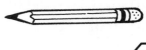 will it take to balance
the scale? Look at the picture. Make a prediction.

about _____ ☐   about _____ ☐

2. Measure each object to check.

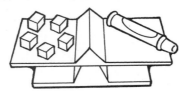   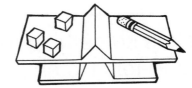

about _____ ☐   about _____ ☐

_____

_ _ _ _ _ _ _ _ _ _ _ _ _ _ _ _ _

3. Which is heavier?   _____

First, make a prediction.
Then, measure to check.

4. Which is heavier, your
sock or your shoe?

_____   _____

_ _ _ _ _   _ _ _ _ _

_____   _____

5. Which is heavier,
1 quarter or 4 nickels?

_____   _____

_ _ _ _ _   _ _ _ _ _

Harcourt Brace School Publishers

Measuring with Cups

Draw a picture.
Solve.

1. A small bowl holds 2 cups of rice. A large bowl holds double this amount. How many cups does the large bowl hold? _____4_____ cups	
2. A carton of juice holds 4 cups. Mrs. Jones buys 2 cartons. How many cups of juice does she buy in all? _____ cups	
3. A blue jug holds 3 cups of milk. A red jug holds 2 cups more. How many cups does the red jug hold? _____ cups	

Mark the correct answer.

4. Which container holds about 1 cup?

Temperature
Hot and Cold

Draw a picture.

1. Jeff plays ball.
   He feels hot.
   Draw something cold for him
   to drink.

2. Sue goes sledding.
   She feels cold.
   Draw something hot for her
   to drink.

3. A jug holds 3 cups of cocoa.
   How many cups will 2
   jugs hold?

   _____ cups

Mark the correct answer.

4. Which is hot?

5. Which is cold?

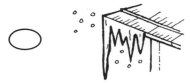

Harcourt Brace School Publishers

Equal and Unequal Parts of Wholes

Draw lines to solve.

1. Kathy and Jane have an orange. They want equal parts. How should they cut the orange?

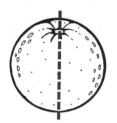

2. Sally and Tom have a sandwich. They want equal parts. How should they cut the sandwich?

3. Four children have a pizza. Each child wants an equal part. How should they cut the pizza?

4. Three children have a cake. Each child wants an equal part. How should they cut the cake?

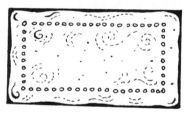

Mark the correct answer.

5. Which figure shows equal parts?

6. Which figure shows equal parts?

PROBLEM SOLVING PS113

Halves

Draw lines to solve.

1. Lily breaks a cracker to show two equal parts or $\frac{1}{2}$. Show how she could break it.

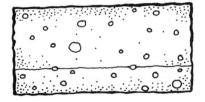

2. Bob and a friend share a pizza. Each gets $\frac{1}{2}$. Show how they could divide it.

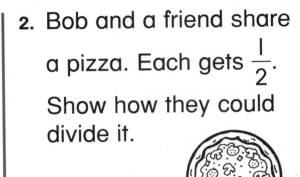

3. Three friends have a large brownie. Each child wants an equal part. How should they cut the brownie?

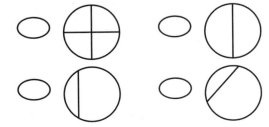

4. 4 children buy a long sandwich. Each child wants an equal part. How should they cut the sandwich?

Mark the correct answer.

5. Which figure shows halves?

6. One of two equal parts is _____.

◯ one half

◯ one whole

Harcourt Brace School Publishers

Fourths

Color the part to solve.

1. Ruth makes a sandwich. She eats $\frac{1}{4}$ for lunch. Show what part she eats.

2. Jeff's mom gives him a fruit bar. He eats $\frac{1}{2}$ for a snack. Show what part he eats.

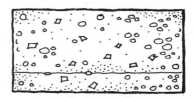

3. Peter picks an apple. He eats $\frac{1}{2}$ for dessert. Show what part he eats.

4. Mary bakes a big pizza. She gives $\frac{1}{4}$ to her friend for a treat. Show what part her friend gets.

Mark the correct answer.

5. Which figure shows fourths?

6. Which part is larger?

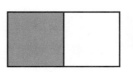

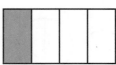

$\frac{1}{2}$ $\frac{1}{4}$

Thirds

Color the part to solve.

1. Toby buys a large cookie at the snack bar. He eats $\frac{1}{3}$. Show what part he eats.

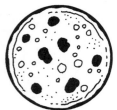

2. Sheila has a big sandwich. She gives $\frac{1}{4}$ to her brother. Show what part her brother gets.

3. Carla has a brownie in her lunchbox. She eats $\frac{1}{3}$ for lunch. Show what part she eats.

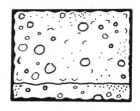

4. Garth buys a pizza. He gives $\frac{1}{2}$ to a friend. Show what part his friend gets.

Mark the correct answer.

5. Which figure shows thirds?

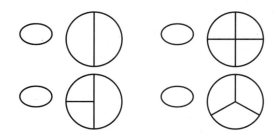

6. A pizza is cut into three equal parts. What do you call one of the equal parts?

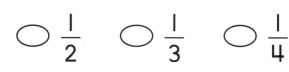

Reading Strategy • Use Visualization

Picturing a problem in your mind can help you solve the problem.

4 children bake a small cake.
Each child gets an equal part.
How should they cut the cake?

1. Read the problem.
   Picture the four children and the cake.

2. Then picture the cake
   divided into 4 equal parts.

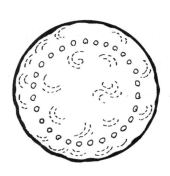

3. Draw lines on the
   cake to show how
   you pictured the cake
   divided into 4 equal parts.

Picture the problem in your mind.
Draw lines to show your picture.

4. There are 3 children in all.
   Each one gets an equal
   share of a pie. How
   should they cut the pie?

5. You want to share a pizza
   with 3 other children.
   How should you cut the
   pizza?

Parts of Groups

Draw and color to solve.

1. Regina has 4 toy cars. I out of 4 of the toy cars is blue. Draw and color the toy cars.	
2. Jose has 3 apples. I out of 3 of the apples is green. Draw and color the apples.	
3. There are 4 children and I pizza. Each child gets an equal share. Draw the pizza.	

Mark the correct answer.

4. Which picture shows I out of 2 of the plums colored?

5. Which picture shows I out of 4 of the berries colored?

Harcourt Brace School Publishers

Sort and Classify

Use the table to solve these problems.

Birds at the Feeder	
blue jay	||||
cardinal	卌 |
bluebird	||

1. How many blue jays did Ann see at the feeder?

   ____4____ blue jays

2. What kind of bird did Ann see most often at the feeder?

   _____

   _____

3. How many birds with blue feathers did Ann see at the feeder?

   _____ birds with blue feathers

4. How would Ann show that another blue jay came to the feeder?

   _____

Mark the correct answer.

5. Which one shows the number 10?

   ◯ 卌 \|\|

   ◯ 卌 \|\|\|

   ◯ 卌 \|\|\|\|

   ◯ 卌 卌

6. How are the birds in Ann's table sorted?

   ◯ by age

   ◯ by color

   ◯ by kind

   ◯ by size

Certain or Impossible

Use the picture.
Color the answer
to each question.

1. Sam is hungry. What can he eat from his bag?

2. Sam wants to buy a snack. What can he use from his bag?

3. Sam wants to color a picture. What can he use from his bag?

4. Sam needs to write. What can he use from his bag?

Mark the correct answer.

5. Which of these things is Sam **certain** to find in his bag?

6. Which of these things is it **impossible** for Sam to find in his bag?

Most Likely

Draw a picture.
Write the answer.

1. A bag has 6 apples and 2 oranges. Jane closes her eyes and takes out a fruit. Which fruit is she most likely to get?

   apple

2. A bag has green grapes and red grapes. Holly wants purple grapes. Can Holly get purple grapes from the bag?

   _____

   _____

   _____

Mark the correct answer.

3. What is your prediction for choosing a ☐ ?

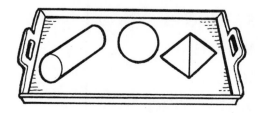

   ◯ impossible

   ◯ certain

4. What is your prediction for choosing a △ ?

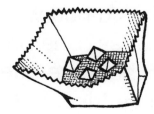

   ◯ impossible

   ◯ certain

Reading Strategy • Use Graphic Aids

You can use a table to help
you solve the problem.

Nicky has a spinner.
She predicts the spinner will stop
on blue more times than red.

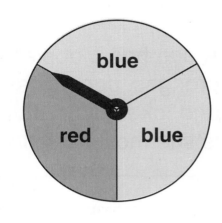

1. Which color do you predict the
   spinner will stop on more often?

   _____

   _ _ _ _ _ _ _ _ _ _ _ _ _ _ _ _ _ _ .

   _____

2. When Nicky spins, she lands on
   blue 7 times and on red 3 times.
   Make a tally mark
   on the table for
   each spin.
   Write the totals.
   Check Nicky's
   prediction.

	Tally Marks	Total
blue		
red		

Solve.

3. Tonia has a bag with 4 red cubes and 8
   white cubes. She predicts she will get a
   white cube more often than a red cube.
   When she tries, she gets red 2 times and
   white 8 times. Is her prediction a good one?

   ◯ yes   ◯ no

Picture Graphs

Favorite Pets					
dog	🐶	🐶	🐶	🐶	
bird	🐦				
fish	🐠	🐠	🐠		
cat	🐱	🐱	🐱	🐱	🐱

Use the graph to answer the questions.

1. How many children in the class choose fish as their favorite pet?

_____3_____ children

2. Write a number sentence that tells how many children like fish and birds best.

____ ◯ ____ = ____

3. 4 more children choose birds as their favorite pet. How many children like birds now?

_____ children

4. The children who like cats and dogs best work together to make a picture. How many children work on the picture?

_____ children

5. Which pet do most children like best?
   - ◯ dog
   - ◯ cat
   - ◯ fish
   - ◯ bird

6. How many children in the class like mice best?
   - ◯ 5 children
   - ◯ 2 children
   - ◯ I child
   - ◯ not here

Reading Strategy • Compare and Contrast

Ramon makes a graph to find out
which fruit his friends like best.

Favorite Fruits						
blueberries						
peaches						
apples						
bananas						

0   1   2   3   4   5   6

1. Look at the graph.
   Compare the colored squares in each row.
   Which fruit has the most colored squares?

   _____

   _____

   _____

2. Which kind of fruit do most children like best?

   _____

   _____

   _____

3. Which kind of fruit do the
   fewest children like?

   _____

   _____

   _____

4. Do more children like
   apples or blueberries?

   _____

   _____

   _____

Harcourt Brace School Publishers

Vertical Bar Graphs

1. Color the graph to match the tally table.

Favorite Colors		Total
Green	II	2
Red	III	3
Blue	I	I

Favorite Colors

```
3
2
1
0
   Green    Red    Blue
```

2. Which color do most children like best?

_____

rⅇⅆ

3. How many more children like green better than blue?

_____ child

4. How many children like red and blue?

_____ children

5. Which color did the fewest children like?

_____

_____

Mark the correct answer.

6. Which number sentence shows how many more children liked red than blue?

○ 3 − I = 2

○ 3 − 2 = I

○ 2 + I = 3

7. How many children in all named their favorite colors?

○ 4 children

○ 5 children

○ 6 children

○ not here

Reading Strategy • Use Graphic Aids

Nancy flips a coin 10 times. She shows what happens in a tally table. Then she makes a graph to show which side of the coin turns up more often.

Nancy's Coin Flips	
heads	||||
tails	卌 |

1. Look at the tally table.
   Count the tally marks and write the totals.

Nancy's Coin Flips		Total
heads	||||	4
tails	卌 |	6

2. Color the graph to match the tally table.

Nancy's Coin Flips						
heads						
tails						

      0   1   2   3   4   5   6

Mark the correct answer.

3. Which side of the coin turned up more often?

   ◯ tails

   ◯ heads

4. Do you think that tails will always turn up more often than heads?

   ◯ yes

   ◯ no

Harcourt Brace School Publishers

Doubles Plus One

Draw a picture. Write the sums.

1. There are 6 bluebirds sitting on
   a fence. Then 7 more join them.
   How many bluebirds are there
   in all?

   $\underline{6} + \underline{7} = \underline{13}$ bluebirds

2. There are 8 crows eating corn.
   Then 9 more crows come.
   How many crows are there
   in all?

   ____ + ____ = ____ crows

3. Tim draws 5 birds.
   Sue draws 6 more birds. How
   many birds do the children
   draw in all?

   ____ + ____ = ____ birds

Mark the correct answer.

4. Which doubles fact can
   help you solve

   $4 + 3 = $ ____?

   ○ $4 + 4$ ○ $5 + 5$
   ○ $7 + 7$ ○ $8 + 8$

5. Which doubles fact can
   help you solve

   $8 + 9 = $ ____?

   ○ $5 + 5$ ○ $6 + 6$
   ○ $7 + 7$ ○ $8 + 8$

Doubles Minus One

Draw a picture. Write the sums.

1. Mrs. Park has 7 stamps. She buys 6 more. How many stamps does she have in all?

   $\underline{7} + \underline{6} = \underline{13}$ stamps

2. Leroy mails 5 letters in the morning and 7 letters in the afternoon. How many letters does he mail in all?

   _____ + _____ = _____ letters

3. Mr. Jones buys 9 baseball stamps and 8 basketball stamps. How many stamps does he buy in all?

   _____ + _____ = _____ stamps

Mark the correct answer.

4. Which doubles fact can help you solve

   $5 + 4 = \underline{}?$

   ○ 3 + 3   ○ 5 + 5
   ○ 7 + 7   ○ 8 + 8

5. Which doubles fact can help you solve

   $8 + 7 = \underline{}?$

   ○ 6 + 6   ○ 9 + 9
   ○ 8 + 8   ○ not here

Harcourt Brace School Publishers

Doubles Patterns

Draw a picture. Solve.

1. A basketball team has 5 players.
Two teams meet for a game, but
I player does not come.
How many players are there?

___9___ players

2. Two baseball teams play a game.
Each team has 8 players. One
team has I extra player. How
many players are there in all?

_____ players

3. A soccer team has 7 players.
Two teams play a game.
I player has to go home.
How many players are left?

_____ players

Mark the correct answer.

4. Which is a doubles-minus-one fact?

○ $9 + 9 = 18$
○ $9 + 7 = 16$
○ $9 + 8 = 17$
○ $9 + 10 = 19$

5. Which is a doubles-plus-one fact?

○ $4 + 4 = 8$
○ $5 + 5 = 10$
○ $5 + 4 = 9$
○ $5 + 6 = 11$

Doubles Fact Families

Draw a picture.
Add or subtract to solve.

1. Steve had 18 marbles.
   He lost 9. How many marbles
   does he have left?

   ___9___ marbles

2. Cindy has 8 rocks. She finds 7
   more. How many rocks does
   she have in all?

   _____ rocks

3. Joe finds 8 shells. Larry finds two
   times as many as Joe. How
   many shells does Larry find?

   _____ shells

Mark the correct answer.

4. Which group of three
   numbers can be used
   to make a doubles
   fact family?

   ○ 4, 4, 8   ○ 4, 6, 8
   ○ 2, 4, 6   ○ 4, 8, 12

5. Which number sentence
   belongs in a doubles
   fact family?

   ○ 6 + 8 = 14
   ○ 7 + 7 = 14
   ○ 14 − 6 = 8
   ○ 14 − 8 = 6

Harcourt Brace School Publishers

Reading Strategy • Use Word Clues

Sal has 3 pencil toppers. Nora has **two times** as many. How many pencil toppers do they have **in all**?

Ken had 16 animal erasers. He **gave some away**. He has 8 left. How many did he **give away**?

1. Read each problem. Look for word clues. Think. How do these words help me decide if I should add or subtract?

2. Use counters to solve each problem. Draw them. Write the answers.

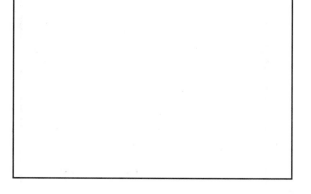

_____ pencil toppers

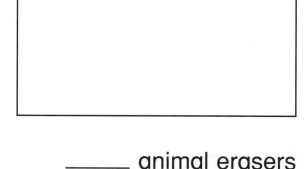

_____ animal erasers

Solve.

3. Jeff has 5 yo-yos. Noah has 1 more than Jeff. How many yo-yos do the boys have in all?

_____ yo-yos

4. Margie had 17 stickers. She gave some away. She has 9 left. How many did she give away?

_____ stickers

Make a 10

Use the make-a-ten strategy to add.
Draw a picture.

1. Ricky has 8 baseball cards.
   He buys 2 more. How many
   cards does he have in all?

   _____10_____ cards

2. Sally has 7 jacks.
   She finds 5 more. How many
   jacks does she have in all?

   _____ jacks

3. Carl has 9 stickers. His sister
   gives him 4 more. How many
   stickers does he have in all?

   _____ stickers

Mark the correct answer.

4. Which fact belongs with
   these facts?

   $2 + 8$ $6 + 4$ $5 + 5$

   ◯ $4 + 5$ ◯ $8 + 1$

   ◯ $7 + 3$ ◯ $9 + 3$

5. Which shows how to use
   the make-a-ten strategy
   to add $6 + 5$?

   ◯ $10 + 1 = 11$

   ◯ $5 + 6 = 11$

   ◯ $5 + 5 + 1 = 11$

Harcourt Brace School Publishers

Sums and Differences to 18

Draw a picture to solve.

1. There are 8 children at the playground. 9 more children come. How many children are at the playground?

   __17__ children

2. 3 children ride bikes. 5 children play on the slide. 7 children swing. How many children are playing in all?

   _____ children

3. There are 17 children at the playground. 8 go home for lunch. How many children are left?

   _____ children

Mark the correct answer.

4. Which strategy could you use to solve this problem?

   $6 + 7 =$ _____

   ○ doubles

   ○ make-a-ten

   ○ doubles plus one

5. What subtraction fact can you figure out by knowing

   $8 + 7 = 15$?

   ○ $15 - 10 = 5$

   ○ $15 - 7 = 8$

   ○ $15 - 9 = 6$

PROBLEM SOLVING   PS135

Counting Equal Groups

Draw a picture.
Write how many in all.

1. Mrs. Jones has 4 window boxes.
   She plants 3 flowers in each box.
   How many flowers in all?

   __12__ flowers

2. Mr. Hill has 3 pots.
   He plants 3 seeds in each pot.
   How many seeds in all?

   _____ seeds

3. Ms. Green has 5 plants.
   Each plant has 2 flowers.
   How many flowers in all?

   _____ flowers

Mark the correct answer.

4. Which picture shows
   2 groups of 3?

   ⬭ not here

5. Which addition sentence
   shows 3 groups of 4?

   ⬭ 4 + 3 = 7

   ⬭ 4 + 4 + 4 = 12

   ⬭ 3 + 3 + 3 + 3 = 12

   ⬭ not here

How Many in Each Group?

Draw a picture.
Solve.

1. Larry feeds 9 bananas to 3 monkeys. Each monkey gets the same number of bananas. How many bananas does each monkey get?

_____3_____ bananas

2. Pam feeds 12 fish to 4 seals. Each seal gets the same number of fish. How many fish does each seal get?

_____ fish

3. Larry feeds 3 goats. He gives them 4 cups of food each. How many cups of food does Larry need?

_____ cups

Mark the correct answer.

4. Which is greater?

  ◯ 3 groups of 4
  ◯ 3 groups of 3

5. Which has more groups?

  ◯ 2 groups of 5
  ◯ 5 groups of 2

How Many Groups?

Draw a picture.
Solve.

1. Art has 12 rolls. He puts 6 rolls in each basket. How many baskets does he use?

   ___2___ baskets

2. Noah has 3 friends. He gives them each 3 crackers. How many crackers does he need?

   _____ crackers

3. Trudy has 8 cookies. She puts 2 cookies on each plate. How many plates does she use?

   _____ plates

Mark the correct answer.

4. Which picture shows 4 groups of 3?

    not here

5. Which addition sentence shows adding 3 groups of 5?

   ◯ $3 + 5 = 8$

   ◯ $5 + 5 + 5 = 15$

   ◯ $3 + 3 + 3 + 3 + 3 = 15$

Harcourt Brace School Publishers

Reading Strategy • Use Word Clues

Using word clues can help
you solve problems.

There are **3** **bowls** of fruit salad. **Each bowl has** 2 red grapes. How many red grapes **in all**?	There are **12** **cherries** and **3 bowls**. How many cherries **in** **each bowl**?	There are **15** green **grapes**. Anna put **5** **grapes in** **each bowl**. **How many bowls** did she use?

1. Read the problem. Look for word clues.

2. Use these word clues to help you.
   Draw a picture. Then solve.

6 red grapes in all	4 cherries in each bowl	3 bowls

Solve.

3. There are 9 crackers.
   Each child gets 3.
   How many children
   get crackers?

   _____ children

4. There are 3 children.
   Each child gets 2 cups of
   juice. How many cups of
   juice in all?

   _____ cups of juice

Adding and Subtracting Tens

Draw a picture.
Find the sum or difference.

1. Mr. Ellis has 50 cows.
   He buys 10 more. How
   many cows does
   he have in all?

   __60__ cows

2. Mrs. Ellis has 90 blocks of
   cheese. She sells 20 blocks.
   How many blocks of cheese
   does she have left?

   _____ blocks of cheese

3. Kathy milks 30 cows.
   Bill milks 20 cows.
   How many more cows
   does Kathy milk?

   _____ more cows

Mark the correct answer.

4. Find the sum.

$$\begin{array}{r} 30 \\ +20 \\ \hline \end{array}$$

  ○ 5   ○ 30
  ○ 50   ○ 55

5. Find the difference.

$$\begin{array}{r} 70 \\ -60 \\ \hline \end{array}$$

  ○ 70   ○ 60
  ○ 50   ○ 10

Harcourt Brace School Publishers

Adding Tens and Ones

Draw a picture.
Find the sum.

1. Ned spends 57¢ on a notebook and 11¢ on a pencil. How much does Ned spend in all?

   <u>68</u> ¢

2. Phil has 50¢ in his pocket. He earns 20¢ more. How much money does Phil have?

   _____ ¢

3. Karen wants to buy 2 cards. Each card costs 30¢. How much money does Karen need?

   _____ ¢

Mark the correct answer.

4. Add.

tens	ones
5	2
+2	6

   ○ 87
   ○ 77
   ○ 78

5. When adding tens and ones, begin by adding the _____ first.

   ○ ones
   ○ tens

Subtracting Tens and Ones

Draw a picture.
Find the sum or difference.

1. Mrs. Jones makes 46 cookies.
   She gives 12 cookies to Tim
   and his friends. How many
   cookies are left?

   __34__ cookies

2. The Cub Scouts make 20 tacos.
   They eat 10 for lunch.
   How many tacos are left?

   _____ tacos

3. Mary makes 24 trail mix bars.
   Paula makes 24 also.
   How many trail mix bars do
   they make?

   _____ trail mix bars

Mark the correct answer.

4. Subtract.

tens	ones
4	5
−3	1

   ○ 76

   ○ 41

   ○ 14

5. When subtracting
   tens and ones, begin
   by subtracting the
   _____ first.

   ○ ones   ○ tens

Reading Strategy • Use Word Clues

Using word clues can help you decide
if an answer to a problem makes sense.

José has **61 shells**.
He finds **12 more**.
How many shells does he have in all?

7 shells   73 shells   730 shells

---

1. Read the problem. Look for word
   and number clues to help you find
   the answer that makes sense.

---

2. Decide if the answer is likely to be
   in the ones, tens, or hundreds.

---

3. Choose the answer that makes sense.

   _____ shells

Mark the answer that makes sense.

4. Mr. Williams has 47
   stamps. He uses 42.
   How many stamps does
   he have left?

   ◯   5 stamps

   ◯   89 stamps

   ◯   500 stamps

5. Alice has 53 marbles.
   She buys 35 more.
   How many marbles she
   have now?

   ◯   88 marbles

   ◯   880 marbles

   ◯   22 marbles